COLLEGE SPORTS TODAY

CAMERON CRAZIES!

THE DUKE BLUE DEVILS STORY

SUE VANDER HOOK

COLLEGE SPORTS TODAY

CREATIVE EDUCATION

Published by Creative Education
123 South Broad Street, Mankato, Minnesota 56001
Creative Education is an imprint of The Creative Company

Designed by Stephanie Blumenthal
Production design by The Design Lab
Editorial assistance by John Nichols

Photos by: Allsport USA, AP/Wide World Photos,
Archive Photos, and UPI/Corbis-Bettmann

Library of Congress Cataloging-in-Publication Data

Vander Hook, Sue, 1949–
Cameron crazies! the Duke Blue Devils story / by Sue Vander Hook.
p. cm. — (College basketball today)
Summary: Examines the history of the Duke University basketball program.
ISBN: 0-88682-988-7

1. Duke Blue Devils (Basketball team)—History—Juvenile literature. 2. Duke University—Basketball—
History—Juvenile literature. [1. Duke Blue Devils (Basketball team)—History. 2. Basketball—History.]
I. Title. II. Series: College basketball today (Mankato, Minn.)

GV885.43.D85V36   1999
796.323'63'09756563—dc21   98-30936

First Edition

2 4 6 8 9 7 5 3 1

It wasn't the national championship game. It wasn't even the Final Four. But it has been heralded as the greatest NCAA tournament game of all time. College basketball fans will never forget the 1992 East Regional finals thriller between Duke and Kentucky. With Kentucky up 103–102 with two seconds left in overtime, Duke forward Grant Hill fired a three-quarters court pass to Christian Laettner. The All-American center took the pass near the foul line, whirled around, and buried an off-balance jumper as the buzzer sounded. The Kentucky crowd stood stunned as jubilant Blue Devils fans stormed the floor. Duke would go on to capture the national championship that year, but that game more than any other characterized the gritty play, hard work, and never-say-die attitude that is the essence of Duke basketball.

CHRISTIAN LAETTNER

CELEBRATES AFTER THE

FAMOUS 1992 SHOT

AGAINST KENTUCKY.

FROM METHODISTS TO DEVILS

Duke University began as a methodist college that was founded in 1850. The school was known as Trinity College until 1928, at which time the name was changed to Duke University in honor of Washington and James Buchanan Duke, father and son tobacco magnates who funded the school and donated much of the land for its campus. With the generous support of the influential Duke family, the school quickly developed a reputation as one of the finest colleges in the Southeast.

The game of basketball has been part of Duke University's rich history for nearly a century. Fifteen years after Dr. James Naismith invented the game in 1891, Duke participated in the first college basketball game ever played in the state of North Carolina, taking on Wake Forest on March 2, 1906. Although Trinity/Duke lost 24–10 that day, the first page of the school's long and illustrious basketball history had been written.

During that first season, the team was coached by Trinity alumnus Wilbur Wade "Cap" Card, the man responsible for introducing the school's students and faculty to the sport of basketball. By Card's fourth season at Trinity, basketball's popularity had grown like wildfire, and his rapidly improving team had posted an 8–1 record.

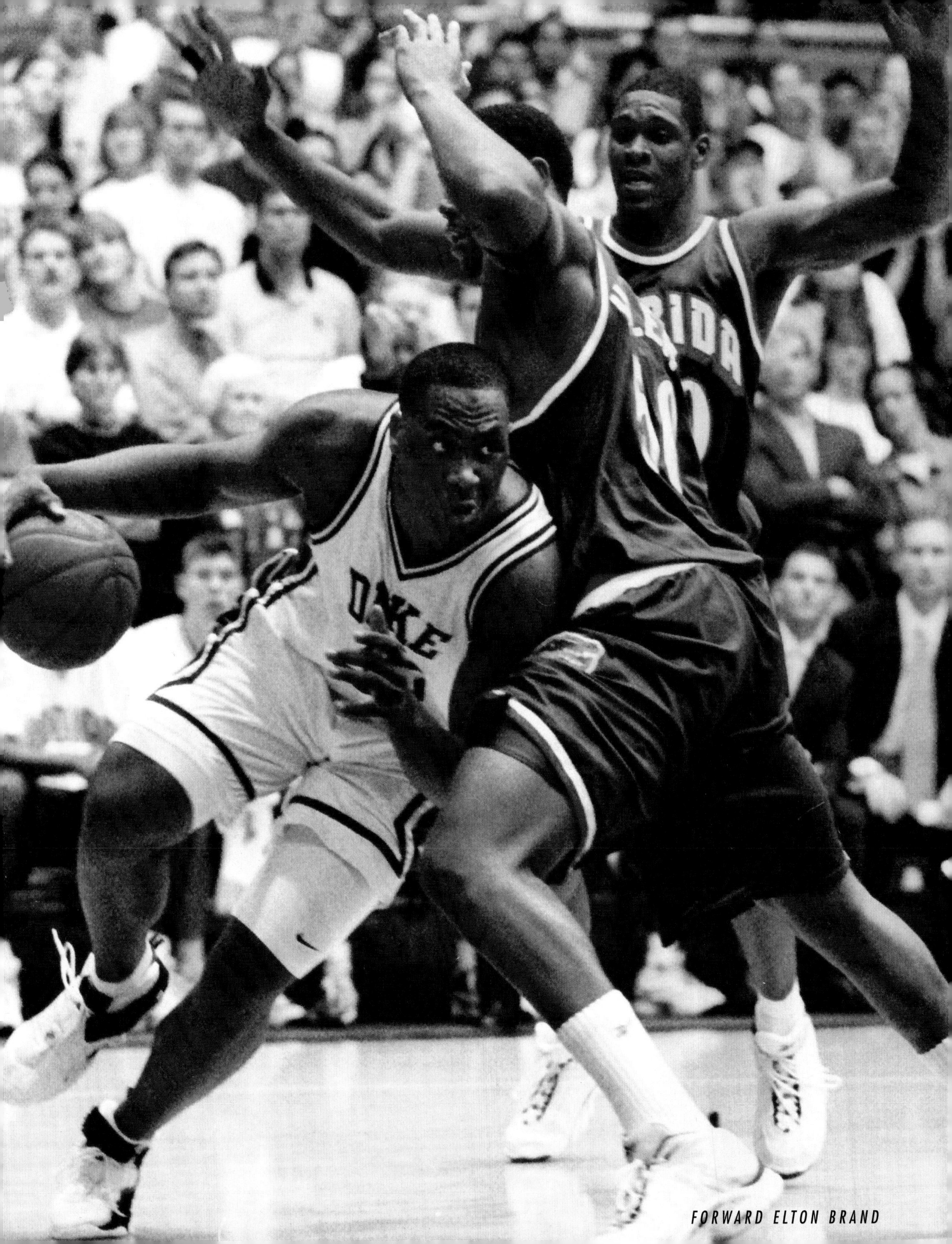

FORWARD ELTON BRAND

THE GREAT JACK MARIN

(ABOVE); ALL-AMERICAN

FORWARD ART

HEYMAN (BELOW)

After Card left Duke in 1912, the basketball program went through 15 years of constant change, led by no less than 10 different coaches from 1913 to 1928. It was during this time that the school's athletic nickname changed from the Methodists to the Blue Devils. Duke hoops truly came into its own when Eddie Cameron took over as the Blue Devils coach. Cameron was hired in 1926 as Duke's freshmen football coach and agreed to serve as the varsity basketball coach as well in 1928.

During Cameron's first season as basketball head man, Duke posted a 12–8 record and made it all the way to the finals of the Southern Conference tournament. During Cameron's reign, the Blue Devils won 226 games and three conference championships and produced the school's first All-Americans in Bill Werber and Bill Mock. These statistics are even more impressive considering Cameron continued to serve as an assistant football coach while leading the basketball team to new heights.

After hanging up his basketball whistle in 1942, Cameron became Duke's head football coach and led the Blue Devils squad to a 25–11–1 record over four seasons and a big win in the 1945 Sugar Bowl. After retiring from coaching in 1946, Cameron served as Duke's athletic director until 1972.

Even today, Cameron's legend surrounds Duke basketball. The Blue Devils' home court, named Cameron Indoor Stadium, was built in 1940 from a design Cameron allegedly sketched on a book of matches. The Duke student section is so loud and boisterous that the fans are affectionately known as the "Cameron

Crazies." As one-time coach Bill Foster said, "His spirit is in everything from the uniforms to the building we play in. He was, and is,
Duke athletics."

DUKE ADDS TO ACC EXCELLENCE

After Cameron stepped down as basketball coach,
the Blue Devils remained a basketball force for the
remainder of the 1940s and '50s behind the performance of
players such as sharpshooting guard Dick Groat, who averaged 23
points a game from 1950 to 1952. Groat went on to an All-Star
career as a professional baseball player and was the first Duke player
to have his jersey (#10) retired.

In 1953, Duke became a charter member of the Atlantic
Coast Conference. Six of the seven schools that forged the ACC
that year still participate in the league. Duke, North Carolina,
Clemson, Maryland, North Carolina State, and Wake Forest
formed the nucleus of what many consider the nation's most
powerful basketball conference. With its nine current teams,
the ACC has compiled a .650 winning percentage in the
NCAA tournament, the best of any major conference.

1953 also signaled the beginning of the ACC tournament, which is today generally considered to be the nation's
premier postseason conference event. Although Duke was

JEFF MULLINS (ABOVE)

AND COACH VIC

BUBAS (LEFT) LED

DUKE IN THE '60S.

GRANT HILL, A THREE-TIME ALL-AMERICAN

eliminated 79–75 in the semifinals of the inaugural tournament by N.C. State, the excitement created by the event set the tone for the tournament's magnificent future. "Doing well in that first tournament was important," said team captain Bernie Janicki. "All the guys felt like we were a part of something special."

Despite posting solid regular-season records, the Blue Devils did not experience much postseason success in the 1950s. Coach Harold Bradley's teams never won the ACC tournament, and the Blue Devils suffered a quick first-round loss after their first berth into the NCAA tournament in 1955. Then, in 1959, a 32-year-old native of Gary, Indiana, named Vic Bubas came to Durham and injected new life into the program.

BUBAS BOOSTS THE BLUE DEVILS

From 1960 to 1967, Bubas's teams ran up the best basketball record in America: 159–37. During those glory years, Duke captured four ACC regular-season titles, three conference tournament championships, and three spots in the Final Four. Driving the success of Bubas's teams were such players as Art Heyman and Jeff Mullins, a dynamic forward duo that combined for an average of 45 points a game in Duke's first-ever run to the Final Four in 1963. The 6-foot-5 and 205-pound Heyman combined a lightning-quick first step with considerable strength to become one of the most feared finishers of his time. "Art Heyman is one of the

FIERCE DEVILS TRAJAN LANGDON (ABOVE) AND ROSHOWN MCLEOD (BELOW)

11

NAME: Jeff Mullins

BORN: July 27, 1944

HEIGHT/WEIGHT: 6-foot-4/185 pounds

POSITION: Forward

SEASONS PLAYED: 1960-61–1963-64

AWARDS/HONORS: All-American (1962-63, 1963-64), 1963-64 ACC Player of the Year, 1964 McKevlin Award winner, 1964 ACC Tournament MVP

Jeff Mullins played under coach Vic Bubas all four of his seasons at Duke, finishing his college career with 1,888 total points. As team captain his senior year, Mullins turned the East Regional Finals into his own personal showcase, scorching Connecticut for 30 points in the title game.

STATISTICS:

Season	Points per game	Rebounds per game
1960–61	–	–
1961–62	21.0	10.4
1962–63	20.3	8.0
1963–64	24.2	8.9

NAME: Vic Bubas

POSITION: Head Coach

SEASONS COACHED: 1959-60–1968-69

AWARDS/HONORS: Three Final Four appearances, Duke Sports Hall of Fame inductee

RECORD: 213–67

After assuming the head coaching position at Duke on May 5, 1959, Bubas made the Blue Devils one of the most dominant teams in the nation for most of the 1960s. This "Duke Decade"— as some have called his reign—included four ACC regular-season championships, four ACC Tournament titles, and three Final Four appearances. From 1960–61 to 1966–67, Bubas's Blue Devils finished among the top 10 teams in the country every season and compiled a 159–37 record—the best in the nation. His career winning percentage of .76 is the best of any Duke coach. Guiding such stars as Jeff Mullins, Art Heyman, and Jack Marin, Coach Bubas continued the tradition of excellence begun by Duke coaching great Eddie Cameron.

PORTRAIT

the great drivers in the game today," declared basketball great Chuck Taylor. "He just overpowers the defense."

Mullins was a 6-foot-4 and 185-pound swingman whose well-rounded game made him dangerous in any situation. The two-time All-American averaged 22 points and nine rebounds per game in his three varsity seasons at Duke. He would later go on to help the Golden State Warriors capture the 1975 National Basketball Association title. "Some do certain things better than Jeff," basketball expert Ron Green once said, "but few do all of them as well." A 94–75 loss to Loyola in 1963 ended Heyman's and Mullins's dream of delivering a national championship to Duke.

The next season, many fans expected Duke to be weakened after Heyman graduated, but Bubas drove his team—centered around Mullins, Jack Marin, and Jay Buckley—to the NCAA finals, where they encountered powerhouse UCLA and legendary coach John Wooden. Bubas's team was overwhelmed by the Bruins, committing 29 turnovers in a 98–83 loss.

In 1966, Bubas found a new star in guard Bob Verga, and the Blue Devils stormed to both the ACC regular-season and tournament championships. With Verga's fantastic floor leadership and

CENTER CHRIS BURGESS WAS PART OF A STRONG ___ COURT IN 1997

19 points-per-game average, the Blue Devils marched to the Final Four once again to face top-ranked Kentucky in the semifinals. Duke fans were confident in their Blue Devils, but their luck ran out when Verga contracted strep throat the week before the game and played sparingly in a 83–79 loss to the Wildcats. For Bubas, the loss was bittersweet. "I wanted to win that game more than anything," he said, "but the effort our young men put out that day made me very proud."

THE "CINDERELLA" DEVILS OF '78

When Bubas stepped down after the 1969 season, Duke was a middle-of-the-pack team for the next five years under coaches Bucky Waters and Neill McGeachy. With the program spinning its wheels, Duke turned to former Utah University coach Bill Foster—a relentless recruiter and advocate of run-and-gun offense—to right the ship.

Unfortunately, during Foster's first three seasons, the gloom of mediocrity continued to hang over the team. The Blue Devils went a combined 5–27 in conference games. Although Foster's job appeared to be on thin ice, he remained optimistic. "I needed time to get some of the players I recruited into the mix," Foster said.

DAN MEAGHER (ABOVE);

JEFF MULLINS, VIC

BUBAS, AND ART HEYMAN

(BELOW, LEFT TO RIGHT)

"I knew these kids were winners—the ACC is just a tough place to grow up."

The kids Foster was referring to were guard Jim Spanarkel, center Mike Gminski, and forward Gene Banks. The relatively unknown threesome began the 1977–78 season with little fanfare; after all, few teams do well in the ACC by relying on a core made up of a junior (Spanarkel), a sophomore (Gminski), and a freshman (Banks). Foster's young stars-in-the-making, however, were too inexperienced to know it.

While the brawny Gminski powered his way to 20 points and 10 rebounds a game, Spanarkel played the role of floor general, posting 19 points a game and passing out 126 assists over the course of the season. The freshman Banks, known as "Tinkerbell" for his high-flying game, used a combination of power moves and a soft shooting touch to average 17 points a game. The awesome athleticism of the "Running Devils" powered Duke to the ACC tournament crown and a berth in the NCAA tournament.

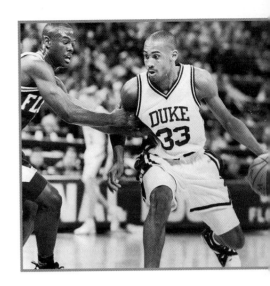

In the big dance, the young Devils hit their stride, posting wins over Rhode Island, Pennsylvania, and Villanova to reach the Final Four. In the semifinals against Notre Dame, the big three of Spanarkel, Gminski, and Banks combined for 71 points in Duke's 90–86 win over the Irish. "I think back on it now and it seems like a dream," Gminski later said. "Everything just seemed to go our way."

In the finals, Duke's Cinderella story finally reached midnight when the powerful Kentucky Wildcats defeated the Devils 94–88, despite 63 points from Foster's "Kiddie Corps" threesome.

The next season, Duke notched a 22–8 mark but was upset in the second round of the NCAA tournament. In 1980, Banks and Gminski powered the Blue Devils to the Elite Eight. After that campaign, however, Foster left to become the head coach at the University of South Carolina, and Duke again was in search of a leader.

COACH K LEADS THE WAY

In seeking a replacement for Foster, Duke officials sought a coach who would both build a winning team and promote the school's high standards for academics and moral character. Coaches like that are not easy to find, but Duke had identified one man who

fit the bill. Mike Krzyzewski had been an assistant under legendary Indiana University coach Bobby Knight and had coached his alma mater, Army, to a 73–59 record from 1976–80.

"I recommended Mike [to Duke officials] because I knew he had it inside him to be a great coach," said Knight. "He looks like an accountant, but he has a fire in his belly and one of the best basketball minds in the game."

Duke turned over the reins of their storied program to the 33-year-old Krzyzewski and has never looked back. But greatness did not come easily to the man Duke fans call "Coach K." When he arrived in Durham, the team had very little talent beyond seniors Gene Banks and guard Kenny Dennard. "People think Mike just walked in and started winning, but when he first got to Duke, the cupboard was pretty bare," former Notre Dame coach Digger Phelps remembered.

Krzyzewski, a former Army captain, immediately implemented a motion offense and an attacking, man-to-man defense, continually drilling his players on fundamentals. After suffering through losing seasons in two of his first three years at Duke, Krzyzewski's methods and recruiting prowess finally began to bear fruit. New stars such as guard Johnny Dawkins, forwards Jay Bilas and David Henderson, and center Mark Alarie all came to Duke in 1982 and turned into a Final Four team by 1986. The Blue Devils, led by the ultra-quick Dawkins's 24 points, beat Kansas and their star, Danny Manning, 71–67 in an exciting semifinals contest. Then, in the finals versus Louisville, Duke's magic season came to an end with a tough 72–69 loss.

RICKY PRICE CONTRIBUTED TO DUKE'S 1996–97 ATTACK WITH NEARLY 10 POINTS PER GAME.

NAME: Grant Hill

BORN: October 4, 1972

HEIGHT/WEIGHT: 6-foot-8/220 pounds

POSITION: Forward

SEASONS PLAYED: 1990-91–1993-94

AWARDS/HONORS: All-American (1991-92, 1992-93, 1993-94), 1993-94 ACC Player of the Year, 1994 All-Final Four selection

Grant Hill, who became an immediate impact player as a freshman, was one of the greatest Blue Devils athletes ever. During his four seasons at Duke, he scored nearly 2,000 points, handed out close to four assists per game, and earned Defensive Player of the Year honors in 1993. For his extraordinary role in two national championships, Hill's jersey was retired.

STATISTICS:

Season	Points per game	Rebounds per game
1990–91	11.2	5.1
1991–92	14.0	5.7
1992–93	18.0	6.4
1993–94	17.4	6.9

NAME: Elton Brand

BORN: March 11, 1979

HEIGHT/WEIGHT: 6-foot-8/260 pounds

POSITION: Forward

SEASONS PLAYED: 1997-98–1998-99

AWARDS/HONORS: All-American (1998-99), 1998-99 National Player of the Year

Brand came to Duke as one of the nation's most sought-after recruits. In 18 starts as a freshman, he ranked third among Blue Devils in scoring and led the team in rebounding. A smooth scorer and a valuable defensive presence, Brand blocked 27 shots and averaged 1.5 steals per game. As a sophomore, Brand established himself as the nation's best player. His dominating performances as a scorer, rebounder, and shot-blocker led Duke to a school-record 32-game winning streak.

STATISTICS:

Season	Points per game	Rebounds per game
1997–98	13.4	7.3
1998–99	17.7	9.8

COACH K LED DUKE TO

A TOP NATIONAL RANKING

FOR MOST OF THE

1998-99 SEASON.

"I'll always have a special place in my heart for those seniors," said the five-time National Coach of the Year. "They set the tone for how Duke basketball is supposed to be played."

Krzyzewski and his 1986 seniors had pushed Duke back into the national spotlight, but it would be a new crop of talent that would keep it there. All-American forward Danny Ferry, savvy point guard Quin Snyder, and defensive stopper Billy King led the charge to another Final Four appearance in 1988. Kansas, however, took its revenge on the Blue Devils, beating Duke 66–59 in the semifinals.

Incredibly, Duke, sparked by the play of freshman phenom Christian Laettner, would return to the Final Four again in 1989.

Laettner and Ferry formed a deadly twosome, but Duke fell in the semifinals once again, losing 95–78 to Seton Hall.

Despite all of Duke's success, the media and many fans began to wonder if Krzyzewski's Devils would ever win the title. For Coach K and his players, the frustration reached its pinnacle in 1990. The Blue Devils featured a young team led by Laettner, a sophomore, and Bobby Hurley, a freshman. Hurley, a whirling dervish of a point guard who barely reached six feet in height, dished out nearly eight assists a game while frustrating opposing ball-handlers with his pesky, tenacious defense.

Laettner, who averaged 16 points and 10 rebounds during the season, was the team's heart and soul. As teammate Thomas Hill once said, the feisty center "had a choirboy's face with an executioner's heart." Laettner led the much-improved Blue Devils into the NCAA tournament, where Duke blew through the field to reach the Final Four once again. After upsetting the heavily favored Arkansas Razorbacks in the semifinals, the Blue Devils were only one step away from the crown.

Fate was not on their side, however, as the inexperienced Devils ran into the powerful Runnin' Rebels of the University of Nevada Las Vegas. The Rebels, led by stars Larry Johnson and Stacey Augmon, used its famed running offense to blow out the Blue Devils 103–73 in the championship game. "We were embarrassed. They ran all over us," said Laettner. "It was painful, but it showed us what it takes to be the best."

VERSATILE ROSHOWN

MCLEOD (ABOVE);

CHRISTIAN LAETTNER

(BELOW)

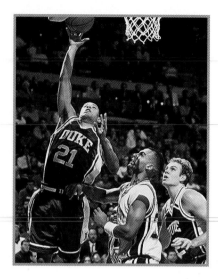

CHAMPIONSHIP GRANT-ED

When a skinny freshman from Reston, Virginia, named Grant Hill participated in his first practice at Duke in 1991, some eyebrows rose. "He didn't look like much," noted forward Greg Koubek. "He was real thin and gangly, but once we started playing, it was easy to see Grant was special."

The son of former Dallas Cowboys Pro-Bowl running back Calvin Hill, Grant had athletic ability to burn. At 6-foot-8, the long-armed, high-flying forward knew no limits as a basketball player. Christian Laettner once told Krzyzewski early in Hill's freshman season, "Grant's the most talented player we've ever had here, and it's not even close." It didn't take long for Hill to prove his skills to Coach K. "Grant Hill is the best player I've ever coached—period," Krzyzewski said. "But he's the reluctant super-star. He wants to be the best, but he doesn't want to separate him-self from the team."

With this superstar-in-the-making added to the already potent mix, Duke broke from the gates fast and never looked back, earning the number-two seed in the Midwest Regional of the NCAA tournament.

After storming through the early rounds, Duke found itself in the Final Four once again. Its opponent in the semifinals would

be a familiar and frightening one—the defending champions from UNLV. "We had to forget about what happened the year before," said Hurley. "We figured we were a whole year better than when they beat us. We couldn't wait for that game to start."

The Devils withstood an early onslaught by the talented Rebels, battling back to trail only 43–41 at the half. "We took their best shot and we were still standing," remembered Laettner. "That really gave us confidence." In the second half, Laettner poured in the last of his 28 points, and the Blue Devils got their revenge, beating UNLV 79–77.

Two days later, behind 18 points from Laettner and 10 from Hill, Duke defeated Kansas 72–65 to capture the school's first-ever national championship. "This is for Coach K," exclaimed junior forward Brian Davis. "It's so great to finally accomplish something he's deserved for a long time."

The next season, Duke returned nearly everyone from its championship squad and went on a rampage that ended with a sparkling 34–2 record and a second national championship. In the NCAA tournament, the Devils used Laettner's miracle shot to squeak by Kentucky in the Eastern Regional finals, then rolled to the title game to face Michigan's famous "Fab Five"—an explosive crew of freshmen players led by forward Chris Webber. The game was close at the half, but Duke, led by Grant Hill's 18 points and

BRILLIANT STRATEGIST

MIKE KRZYZEWSKI

(ABOVE); CENTER

CHEROKEE PARKS (BELOW)

10 rebounds, pasted Michigan's highly touted fivesome in the second half, winning 71–51.

In 1993, with two national championships under his belt and teammates Laettner and Hurley playing professionally, many thought that Grant Hill would leave Duke for the NBA as well. But Hill, taught by his parents to always have a "second parachute" in life, stayed for his senior year and got his bachelor of arts degree in political science.

The superstar forward capped his spectacular Duke career by carrying the Blue Devils to the 1994 NCAA finals. This time Duke would fall short, losing 76–72 to Arkansas, but the three-time All-American gave it his all, scoring 12 points, ripping down 14 rebounds, and handing out six assists. "Grant is just a supremely gifted basketball player," said Krzyzewski. "There is nothing he can't do."

FEISTY DUKE GUARDS

BOBBY HURLEY (ABOVE)

AND STEVE

WOJCIECHOWSKI (BELOW)

A NEW DYNASTY

Most experts figured that Duke's biggest obstacle during the 1994–95 season would be overcoming the loss of superstar Grant Hill. As it turned out, Duke fans would face an even bigger loss that season. Suffering from terrible back pain and exhaustion, Coach Krzyzewski was forced to leave the team after 12 games to have back surgery. After a 9–3 start under Krzyzewski,

WILLIAM AVERY HELPED

CONTINUE THE DUKE

TRADITION OF EXCELLENCE

IN THE LATE '90S.

the inexperienced Blue Devils struggled without their leader, finishing the season 13–18 and missing a postseason berth.

Krzyzewski returned refreshed the following season, and by 1998, he had Duke back on top of the ACC. Gritty pointman Steve Wojciechowski, sweet-shooting guard Jeff Capel, high-flying forward Roshown McCleod, and versatile guard Trajan Langdon spurred Duke to the regular-season conference title and a trip to the Sweet 16 of the NCAA tournament.

In 1998–99, Duke was back with a vengeance. Powerful center Elton Brand, bruising forward Shane Battier, smooth point guard William Avery, and skywalking swingman Corey Maggette formed one of Duke's most potent lineups ever. After a 5–1 start, the Blue Devils roared through the rest of the schedule without a loss, blowing out opponents by more than 25 points per game.

In the NCAA tournament, it appeared that nothing could stop Duke, as the top-ranked Devils easily advanced to the Final Four, then dispatched a physical Michigan State squad to earn a shot at their third national title of the decade. Duke's fabulous ride continued as Elton Brand—who would leave for the NBA after the season—was named the National Player of the Year one day before the title game.

The Blue Devils' opponent would be Connecticut, the only team besides Duke to spend time at the top of the rankings during the season. Although senior guard Trajan Langdon netted 25 points for the Devils, UConn All-American Richard Hamilton countered with 27 points of his own to lead the Huskies to a thrilling 77–74 upset victory. The loss left Duke with 37 wins—one shy of a new NCAA record.

The defeat was tough to take, but Coach Krzyzewski proudly focused on his team's fantastic season. "[We're] disappointed about what didn't happen," he said about the final loss. "But what did happen was unbelievable." With the ever-optimistic Coach K leading his troops into the new millennium, these Devils may soon reach heavenly heights once again.